SEPARATION AND DIVORCE IN NORTH CAROLINA

Mary K. Nicholson

Foreword

According to the North Carolina Department of Vital Statistics, 34,039 couples either divorced or got annulments in 1990 in North Carolina. A greater number of couples are expected to divorce in 1992 and future years. Divorce has an emotional social and economic impact on the couples, their children and extended families. Divorce now has as great an impact on our lives and society as have birth and death. As a result, the legal relationship of parties to a divorce is as complicated as the legal rights attached to birth and death. While most individuals have traditional concepts of inheritance and general legal rights associated with birth and death, the legal rights and obligations associated with separation and divorce are not as commonly known or understood.

This book is not intended to substitute for the advice of an attorney. Even though your particular situation may be the same or similar to the theoretical facts in this text, you should consult an attorney so he or she can review your individual situation.

I wrote this book to attempt to answer, in a general fashion, questions which people repeatedly asked me professionally and socially. I hope its text will help familiarize you with some of the applications of the law in North Carolina domestic situations. With that familiarity, I hope you will better be able to communicate with your lawyer and your spouse. If you have children, I hope that they will benefit from that communication.

Table of Contents

Chapter 1 – Separation

Chapter 2 – Annulment

Chapter 3 – Divorce

Chapter 4 – Property Settlement and Debt

Chapter 5 – Alimony

Chapter 6 – Child Support

Chapter 7 – Custody and Visitation

Chapter 8 – Stepparents

Chapter 9 – Attorney Fees

Definitions

Appendixes

CHAPTER 1
SEPARATION

Separation is the beginning of the legal issue known as divorce. People ask if they are legally separated. This question, by itself, cannot receive a yes or no answer.

When am I legally separated?

Separation in North Carolina is accomplished in different manners for different purposes.

Let's take a hypothetical couple, John and Mary. If they establish separate residences and hold themselves out as being separated without resuming the marital relationship for one year, then they can obtain an absolute divorce. They are legally separated from the date they quit living together for the purpose of obtaining a final divorce.

So, separation by living separate and apart is one form of legal separation. A second form of legal separation would be the execution by the parties of a written agreement called a separation agreement. This agreement is most commonly drawn up by an attorney and covers custody, support, alimony, and property division.

The third type of separation is a court-ordered separation called a "divorce from bed and board," which should not be confused with a final divorce.

Do I need a separation agreement to get a divorce?

In our example, John and Mary have not resolved issues of support or property. Obtaining a divorce without resolving these issues can result in the waiver of rights to property, support or other matters. Claims for division of property must be asserted at the time of divorce. If one spouse sues for divorce and the other spouse does not respond with a claim for division of property that spouse waives the right to claim a division of marital property.

If John and Mary simply quit living together, John and Mary would be separated but subject to claims for alimony in the same manner as during the marriage. Alimony is discussed in another chapter.

A second form of separation is what most people mean when they are "legally separated." This form is the entering of the parties into an agreement called a separation agreement. More properly, a separation agreement is usually a separation and property agreement. The parties in this agreement determine such things as property rights, pension rights, payment of debts, inheritance rights, child custody, support and visitation, and possession and division of property and monies.

When can I date?

I am often asked if a person can "date" after a separation agreement is entered. The same question is asked when people simply separate by establishing separate residences. The answer depends upon the likelihood of one party asserting or prevailing in an alimony claim against the other party. Certainly, a party who would otherwise be subject to such a claim is in a better position with an agreement. However, an agreement does not mean that a claim will not be made by the other party. Ask Donald Trump about agreements. The law in North Carolina is not altogether clear on the matter. You should discuss this with your lawyer.

By the term "date," people mean anything from going to a movie or dinner, to having sex or living with a person who is not his or her spouse. Emotions seem to be provoked in the estranged spouse when this occurs and you should be well versed in what your position is legally and what you have to lose by your conduct.

These papers say I have a divorce from bed and board. Why is that not a divorce?

A third form of separation is a court-ordered separation. The legal term is often confused with an absolute divorce, but is not the same. A court-ordered separation is legally termed as a "divorce from bed and board." It affects the inheritance and possessory rights of the parties. One spouse may be ordered to leave the residence. Claims for temporary alimony are often asserted at this time, as well as claims for child support and custody.

However, a divorce from bed and board is simply a court-ordered separation, not a final divorce.

When do we divide property?

Property division in North Carolina, if not agreed on by the parties, is determined at the end of the year's waiting period for absolute divorce. Possession of properties pending that division may be made by the court at an earlier time.

Pending the end of the year's separation, the court may order one party or the other to retain possession of marital property.

If you get mad at your spouse and sell or destroy or dispose of property, you will probably have to account for its value from your share of the division of property.

In certain circumstances, a partial distribution of marital property can be made before the year's separation period. A court can make a partial distribution if one spouse can show that the other is in control of the bulk of the marital property and the other spouse is in need of his or her portion for necessities and certain other expenses, or is in a position of economic disadvantage with the other spouse.

How long will it take to get a court-ordered separation agreement?

Suppose that John and Mary cannot agree on the terms of a separation agreement. Mary's lawyer suggests that the cost in attorney fees will probably be more than Mary wants to spend to reach a settlement, and if John and she cannot agree, they will end up in court with that expense anyway. Mary decides to go to court. She serves John with papers called a "Complaint" seeking possession of the home, custody of the children, temporary and permanent alimony and possession of the household goods and furnishings until a permanent division of property can be made by the court. Mary may receive all, or none, or a part of her demands.

In this situation, if John had physically abused Mary and presented an immediate threat to her or the children, it would be more obvious that the parties would have extreme difficulty reaching an agreement, although some parties can agree even in those circumstances. Mary could have requested an emergency order and if allowed by the court, she could have had John removed from the home and kept away. In the emergency order situation, John would have been entitled to have the judge hear his side within ten days.

While an emergency order can be issued without notice, a hearing as to possession of the home under an ordinary complaint could not be held for at least ten days, and usually takes longer, depending on how many cases the judge has to head. John and Mary could foreseeably live in the house together for that time. Sometimes a written agreement is reached for one or the other to leave.

Can I move out of the house?

Both parties should always consult a lawyer prior to leaving the marital home for another residence. When a spouse leaves the house, claims may arise for alimony. You need to talk to your lawyer to see if you are at risk for those potential claims.

What happens if we "get back together?"

It is no longer the law in North Carolina that one sexual liaison between estranged spouses voids the separation. And a reconciliation does not set aside all property provisions of a separation agreement. The standard at the time of this writing is that the parties must hold themselves out as being husband and wife to stop the running of the year's separation period.

Reconciliation subsequent to the entering of a separation agreement is much more complicated in terms of the property rights of the parties and rights arising out of the marriage, such as inheritance and claims for support. Once parties enter a separation agreement, they need to see a lawyer to make sure they know their rights. You may need to enter an agreement revoking the prior agreement. It may be to one or the other's individual advantage to let some provisions of the agreement stand by operation of law. You should consult an attorney to find out exactly what your position is if you have entered a separation agreement and are now reconciled.

For example, Mary and John had separated in 1982 and had entered a separation agreement at that time. John had deeded his interest in the home to Mary pursuant to the terms of the separation agreement. The agreement said it was a property settlement and separation agreement and that the terms of the property settlement were separate and apart from the provisions as to other terms of the agreement. John also agreed to pay Mary alimony of $900 a month.

In 1983, John and Mary got back together and lived in the house until their subsequent separation and divorce in 1992. At that time, John claimed he had a marital interest in the home. Mary claimed he did not and that the home was her property under the terms of the old separation agreement. Mary was correct.

Mary also claimed John owed her alimony under the terms of the old separation agreement and that he should begin paying her the $900 a month since they were no longer living together. John claimed he did not have to pay her the money under the old agreement. John was correct.

The difference in the alimony and the house is that the alimony was to be paid in the future and the house was a completed transaction.

Was it truly a reconciliation?

Death of a spouse prior to absolute divorce may bring up this issue. The deceased may have children from another marriage who feel that the estranged or formerly estranged spouse is now claiming a reconciliation solely to get more money. The rights of the children and spouse in these cases have to be either settled or sorted out by the courts. The agreement has to be interpreted both in light of the law's application to the property provisions and the factual circumstances surrounding the alleged reconciliation. The spouse and the children should consult lawyers and provide the lawyers with a definitive list of assets to see what is actually at stake prior to embarking on a long litigation. It may be cheaper to settle or it may be to the spouse's advantage not to pay the lawyer to proceed. In other words, how much money is at stake?

Although these situations are emotionally charged, the lawyer must deal with the legal aspects of the case. If you choose to pursue a case on principle, regardless of the reality of the circumstances, you will probably find it expensive.

Is the date we quit living together important?

Yes. The date of separation determines the property rights of the spouses and the values of property. If Mary came to my office and told me she had definitely decided to leave John but she was unsure of when she wanted to leave, one of the questions I would ask her would be if John was vested in any pension rights with his employer. If Mary and John separated before John's pension vested, Mary would have no right to the pension. If the pension was vested, it would be marital property and Mary would have a right to the portion acquired during the marriage. The term "separated" does not necessarily refer to the date of a separation agreement but can mean the date John and Mary quit living together as husband and wife.

CHAPTER 2
ANNULMENT

Annulment of marriages is only granted upon certain, limited grounds, Historically, under English law, divorce was only granted on limited grounds. Often, one spouse would consent to the accusation to obtain the desired result.

Can I get an annulment?

Clients, especially those with a very brief marriage, want to know if they can get an annulment and not endure the year's waiting period to obtain an absolute divorce in North Carolina.

The grounds for an annulment are as follows:

(1) Persons nearer of kin than first cousins, or between double first cousins.

(2) Male person under sixteen years of age.

(3) Female person under sixteen years of age.

(4) Persons already married with a living spouse.

(5) Physical impotency.

(6) Incompetent and unable to contract from a lack of capacity.

(7) False representation of pregnancy prior to the marriage, followed by a separation of the parties

within forty-five days of the marriage, and continuous separation for one year, unless a child shall have been born to the parties within ten lunar months of the date of separation.

Annulment is not common due to the provisions for uncontested divorce. In most cases, it is less expensive to wait for the divorce. Some persons seek an annulment as a result of religious beliefs. North Carolina's current property distribution laws may generate more requests for annulments if parties seek to avoid designation of property as marital property subject to division.

CHAPTER 3

DIVORCE

In North Carolina, an absolute divorce may only be obtained after a one-year separation. The party seeking the divorce must be a resident of North Carolina for at least six month priot to filing for divorce, and must have lived continuously separate and apart from the other spouse for one year.

When does the year start running?

A client asked me recently if the one-year time period for divorce runs from the date the spouses stop living together or from the later date of the separation agreement. The answer is that the one-year time period runs from the date the spouses cease living together as husband and wife.

Although your lawyer may ask you if you have had intercourse with your spouse in the last year, an isolated instance of sexual intercourse will not interrupt the running of the one-year period. If the parties hold themselves out as man and wife, the year is interrupted. For instance, John and Mary check into a hotel room as man and wife with the idea of reconciliation, but John gets angry and leaves the next morning. John and Mary, in this example, have created havoc with their year's separation and possibly a separation agreement, if they have one.

Does the sheriff have to come out to serve papers?

When one spouse sues for divorce, the sheriff generally serves the Complaint for divorce on the other spouse.

A spouse being sued can accept service of the papers by going to the office of the other party's attorney. I generally do not like this practice and I particularly do not like spouses of clients accepting service if no other attorney is involved. I find acceptance of service creates delay.

In some cases, the spouse is served with the papers by registered mail. The spouse who receives the papers must decide, at this time, if they want to claim alimony or property distribution. If you have a claim for either, you should immediately contact a lawyer. You will waive those rights if you do not respond in a timely fashion.

Can I file my own divorce?

I see many people in court today representing themselves in divorce actions. I advise people to get an attorney to make sure they are not waiving their rights to property. Remember that pensions and marital property are subject to distribution claims.

An attorney also makes sure the judgment is

entered properly. I believe that, generally, persons who do the paperwork for their own divorce have problems with the final decree. In the past few years, the cost of attorney fees has decreased for the filing of divorces and I am sure that the money spent is worth the service. Particularly if the attorney determines that a property right exists that was unknown to you.

Property rights include pensions, Social Security, IRA's and other retirement and profit-sharing benefits. Also included in property rights are claims to bank accounts even if they are in the sole name of the other spouse. Land and leases are also property rights. Debts are subject to division even if incurred in the name of one spouse or the other spouse. You must assert these rights prior to divorce or you will waive them.

Just because your spouse asks for a division of property in the Complaint, does not mean you are entitled to a division if your spouse drops his or her claim after divorce. You must assert your right to division prior to a judgment of divorce. Both parties need to assert this right in writing in a proper manner and file with the court.

How long will it take to get an uncontested divorce?

Approximately 45 days. A divorce is like any other civil action and the same rules of court apply. Once the papers are filed, they have to be served on the other spouse. After the other spouse receives the papers, he or she has 30 days to respond and then the matter can be set for a hearing before a judge. Depending on the rules in the county clerk's office, the case probably will be heard within two to three weeks of the expiration of the 30-day response time.

The spouse who has been served with papers can waive the 30-day response time. The waiver must be in writing and filed with the court.

John and Mary had this problem when they married. John had a previous marriage when he was 17. John had failed to get a divorce even though the marriage had lasted only a few weeks. John filed for divorce and Mary planned their wedding. The invitations were sent out and the date for the wedding set. Mary and John did not know that it would take 45 days to get his divorce decree. Mary and John could not even get a marriage license without the decree. John and his first wife were on good terms and generally blamed the failed marriage on having married too young. John called his first wife and told her that he was planning to remarry and he wanted to get the divorce as soon as possible. John's first wife was cooperative and agreed to go to a lawyer to sign a waiver of the 30-day response period.

Do I have to go to court to get a divorce?

No. North Carolina has adopted a procedure whereby a divorce can be obtained without either party appearing in court. I prefer the practice of having one spouse come to court for a short examination. I have had clients raise concerns about their property or other rights in court that they had completely failed to mention previously. A certain finality also occurs when the person seeking the divorce is present. However, if you choose not to go to court, make sure a final judgment is signed and you receive a copy.

How soon after my divorce can I remarry?

It depends. An absolute divorce is a civil action which like any other civil action is subject to appeal. A spouse has 30 days to appeal the judgment of divorce. Absolute divorce judgments are rarely appealed. A divorced spouse could be married as soon as a certified copy of the divorce judgment is obtained. If notified in advance, the clerk usually can prepare a certified copy the day of the divorce decree. However, if an appeal is filed and the marriage takes place, the newlyweds may have to remarry.

CHAPTER 4
PROPERTY SETTLEMENT AND DEBT

Property settlements

Property settlement can be made by agreement or it can be made by the courts. Before you enter an agreement, you should consult a lawyer as to your rights under North Carolina's Equitable Distribution Act. Interpretation by the courts of that legislation causes changes that you may need to know.

North Carolina is not a "community property" state, but it does have a statute which defines separate property and marital property. Some examples of separate property are:

(1) Property acquired by a spouse before marriage.

(2) Property acquired by a spouse by inheritance.

(3) Property acquired by gift during the course of the marriage. Note that if the gift is from the other spouse, evidence must be produced of intention to make a gift. Written evidence will probably be required. Save those cards and gifts.

Is the property I owned before we got married still mine?

Property owned by one spouse prior to the marriage and later invested in property titled in both names can be traced to separate property. Be careful with real estate. You should consult your attorney especially when putting land or a home in joint names. There is a presumption of a gift.

For example, John inherited various tracts of land and some money, both before and after the marriage. John then bought or traded inherited real estate and money for other tracts of land. Additionally, some portions of the new tracts were paid for partially with money John made after the marriage. In each purchase after the marriage, John had the property deeded to himself and Mary. When they divorced, John claimed that he was at least entitled to claim as separate property the tracts purchased with the money he inherited. Mary claimed the property was marital property and she was entitled to half of it. Mary was correct. John is presumed to have made a gift to Mary when he titled the real property in both names.

Another example. Say that John had been in military service in Vietnam and had saved his money. John had $10,000 in a savings account when he married Mary. Mary and John then opened a joint account and John put his $10,000 in the account and both Mary and John deposited amounts in the account from their earnings. Over the marriage, amounts were withdrawn for living expenses, vacations, and family emergencies. The current balance in the account is

$40,000. John claims he is entitled to his original $10,000. John has a hard row to hoe here. This account is beginning to look like marital property.

However, John also had a stock account with a $5,000 value in stock when he and Mary were married. He has sold stock on several occasions and bought other stock with the money earned. He has a record of the transactions and it is clear that no additional monies have gone into the account. John has no special expertise or knowledge of stock and has spent little time or effort in these transactions. It appears that any increase in value has been through increase in value of the stock over the years. The stock account is now worth $30,000. John has a good chance of having this property declared separate property. Obviously, the original $5,000 is his individual property. The court will have to look at the appreciation in value in relation to his contribution during the marriage to that increase. If John had been a stock broker, it would be clearer that this account was partially marital property because it was an increase related to an expertise exercised during the marriage, i.e., "it was a job" as opposed to an investment.

If the property is titled in my name, isn't it mine?

Property acquired after the marriage which qualifies as marital property is subject to division no matter if it is titled in an individual spouse's name or both names.

John has a lot at Holden Beach. Mary did not want to buy the lot and thought it was a foolish investment. John bought the lot, titled it in his name, and paid for it from his salary. Mary hates fishing and the coast. These transactions have always been a "sore thumb." The lot was purchased for $3,000 and is now worth $40,000. The boat is worth about $12,000. Mary says she is entitled to one-half of these assets. She is right. If John chooses to keep these assets, he will have to give Mary $26,000 in other assets.

John and Mary's house is now worth $150,000, with a $20,000 mortgage. John and Mary have equity of $130,000. Each is entitled to $65,000 equity from the house. John may choose to give Mary $26,000 of his equity for the lot and boat.

However, Mary has "banked" her salary during the marriage. John wanted to pay all the expenses from his salary. Mary felt she was entitled to keep her own money if she worked. Mary's bank accounts are all in her own name and John does not even know how much money is deposited in those accounts. John gets mad and tells Mary he is claiming one-half of her bank deposits because she made a claim on his boat. John will get one-half the deposits because they are marital property.

What is marital property?

Marital property is property acquired by other than individual gift or inheritance between the date of the marriage and the date of the separation. Note this is the date of the separation, not the absolute divorce.

Here are some examples of marital property:

(1) Vested pensions, or at least the portion accrued during the marriage.

(2) Military pensions, in some cases.

(3) Certificates of deposit and savings acquired during the marriage by other than gift or inheritance.

(4) The equity in a home if acquired during the marriage by other than gift or inheritance. Remember to consult your lawyer about the title to the house. If you deed it to her or him, or Daddy or Mama deeds it to her or him, it may be a gift.

(5) Automobiles purchased during the marriage.

(6) Also the boat you bought.

(7) The furniture purchased during the marriage, including appliances, televisions, stereos, etc.

Many other examples exist, but I am sure you are getting the idea. All that seems pretty clear until property takes on a combined character, such as the joint bank account of Mary and John.

Another example of a combined character is when an asset held prior to the marriage is improved during the marriage by the effort of both parties or one party or the other during the marriage.

Let's say that John and Mary had built a rental

house on a lot John bought prior to their marriage. The house was built after the marriage and a mortgage was incurred to build the house. Although John never deeded the land to himself and Mary, Mary had to sign the Note and Deed of Trust. The mortgage was paid by rent and by funds earned by both parties during the marriage. The lot was purchased by John for $10,000. The mortgage was for $30,000. The lot is now worth $50,000 and the house is worth $80,000, without land value. The problem here is to determine how much of the increase in value is marital property and how much is John's separate property.

Had John deeded the lot to himself and Mary, there would be a presumption of a gift and the increase in value would be marital. This presumption of a gift would not exist if the property were not land.

He gave it to me, isn't it mine? Or, my parents gave it to us, isn't it mine?

Gifts raise another issue. In order for gifts between spouses to be individual property not subject to division, the "intention must be stated in the conveyance." A deed to land seems to be sufficient without any other written indication of gift. Check with an attorney to find out the exact status in this area. It is unclear at best and can create lawsuits over the nature of the property and whether it is subject to division.

Gifts from parents to a child are the property of that individual. If John's parents had deeded a lot to

John and Mary to build a house, Mary would probably prevail in claiming this was a gift to her and John and, therefore, marital property. However, if John had inherited his parents' home, that home would clearly be separate property. If John took his funds acquired during the marriage to improve that home, the improvements and increases in value related to those improvements would be subject to division.

Don't I get one-half of the property?

While there is a presumption that the division of marital assets is equal, a court can make an unequal division based upon factors which include the need of a parent with custody of a child or children of the marriage to occupy or own the marital residence and to use or own its household effects. The presumption is for an equal division. Either party may show a reason why the division should be other than equal.

Debts

Marital debts also must be divided. Debts, just like property, can be divided by agreement of the parties or by order of court.

What happens if he doesn't make the car payment and my name is on the loan?

John and Mary decided to enter into a separation agreement. The agreement provided that John make the payment on his 1986 Corvette. Both Mary and John had signed the note when the car was purchased. John bought the car in 1990 and the payments were scheduled to continue for another four years. John agreed to make the car payment in the agreement.

John and Mary did not fully realize that establishing two households was going to be such an expense. John could not keep up regular payments on the car and it was repossessed. The car was sold by the lender, but did not bring a price sufficient to cover the remaining debt. The lender sued John and Mary for the $2,000 difference between what was owed on the car and what the lender received for the car when it was sold. Mary is now furious because she mistakenly believed her obligation to pay the debt had ended when John agreed to pay it.

The separation agreement is a contract between two parties. This agreement does not relieve the parties of obligations to creditors. The creditors are not a party to this agreement and their rights are not affected by the agreement.

Some agreements provide that a party who does not pay, must repay the party who suffers a loss as a result of the failure of the other party. These provisions can be difficult to enforce especially if the defaulting party has no ability to pay in the first place. You should also be aware that the type of default described with John and Mary will appear on both's credit ratings.

Am I responsible for his debts?

In general, creditors cannot hold one spouse responsible for the debts of another spouse.

In cases of a court-ordered division of property and payment of debt, enforcement of the order is possible. Parties under a court order can be held subject to the contempt powers of the court if they fail to abide by the order and have an ability to pay the debt.

In cases of mental and physical disability, an obligation of support may arise. You should immediately consult a lawyer if you foresee this situation arising. Long-term disability can create both legal and financial problems for spouses. In some cases, the parties find it necessary to obtain a divorce to survive the financial burden.

Can his creditors take the house?

Yes or no, depending upon how the house is deeded and whether both spouses owe the debt.

In North Carolina, land and a home on that land, or real property, is owned as tenants by the entirety if it is purchased by married persons and titled in their joint names. Among other things, this designation as a tenancy by the entirety protects jointly owned real property from execution and sale by creditors of an individual spouse.

However, once a final divorce judgment is entered, the real property is no longer protected by joint ownership. A creditor who has got a judgment against one spouse can seek to force the sale of the property to get payment.

For example, John and Mary owned a tract of land in Wilkes County. John and Mary borrowed money on the property and signed papers putting the property up as security for the debt.

John owed money to Jim Jones for a bad business venture. Jim Jones sued John and was awarded a judgment by the court for $25,000. John had been afraid to tell Mary about the business venture and the debt because he knew she would have a fit over his taking such a risk. Mary was not sued and had no liability for the debt to Jim Jones. Since Mary and John owned their home as tenants by the entirety, or married persons, Jim Jones could not attempt to force a sale of the house.

When Mary found out about the debt and judgment, Mary and John separated and divorced a year later. Mary decided not to go to a lawyer and to sell the house when the market got better. John said he would give the money to Mary when the house was sold. At closing, Mary discovered that the judgment against John would have to be paid from his half of the property since they were divorced and no longer held the property as a tenancy by the entirety.

After the divorce, if Jim Jones had decided to force a sale of the property to collect his money, he could have done so. In many cases, a creditor does not force the sale because there is a mortgage on the property and the debt is as much or greater than the value of the property.

Another common concern is when the residence of the parties is transferred to one spouse. The other spouse may want his name taken off the debt. Unless the spouse who receives the property is willing to, or more often, able to refinance the property, the other spouse cannot have his name removed from the debt unless the mortgage lender consents.

A foreclosure on the property would therefore affect the credit of both spouses. If a spouse steps in to pay the debt to preserve credit the property does not automatically revert to the spouse who paid the debt. An indemnity agreement can be set forth in a separation agreement. However, if the defaulting spouse cannot pay the mortgage, he or she generally has difficulty reimbursing the other spouse.

In the transfers of real property, veterans should consult the Veterans Administration as to their eligibility for a new loan if their existing VA loan is not paid off.

Chapter 5
Alimony

Can I take him for everything I can get?

To do that, you have to be prepared for several things, one of which is a large attorney fee. If, in fact, you receive temporary alimony, you may receive reimbursement for a portion of that fee. You may receive no reimbursement. Your spouse is only obligated to pay attorney fees if you have an inability to pay the fee and cannot prosecute your action on an equal footing.

In our earlier example of John and Mary, John has confessed to Mary that he is having an affair with the only true love of his life, Susie. Susie is a twenty-one-year-old flight attendant. John, has moved out of his home with Mary and the children and moved into a condominium owned by Susie.

Mary has a near permanent collapse when he informs her of his relationship with Susie. When she recovers, she gets mad and goes to see a lawyer. Not only does she want alimony from John, she wants him to pay the legal expenses from her alimony claim.

However, Mary has $30,000 in a savings

account. The $30,000 was Mary's inheritance from her parents. At this stage, it appears Mary has sufficient means to pay her attorney and probably will not recover those expenses from John even if she wins and receives alimony.

While alimony is no longer always paid from the husband to the wife, it is still generally paid in that fashion. For the purposes of this chapter, I will use he and she in that fashion to avoid confusion. Most examples can be reversed if you are a husband seeking alimony.

Can I get alimony?

Alimony is not what it was to women in the past. Now, in North Carolina, a spouse who is not dependent on her husband is not eligible for alimony. Dependency may mean that the spouse is unable to live at her accustomed standard of living, and not just that she can provide herself with food, shelter, and clothing. One case has held that a $10,000 difference in annual salary was sufficient for dependency. Cases where the husband and wife make about the same amount of money with no other income generally do not create a dependency. Lack of dependency means the wife will not receive permanent alimony. Temporary support during the year's separation may be another situation.

Spouses seeking temporary support should also realize that if they are not awarded permanent support, they may be ordered to pay back the temporary support they have received.

How long do I have to pay her all this money?

Alimony is support usually in the form of monthly payments from one spouse to another until the spouse receiving alimony dies or remarries. Court orders for alimony are subject to review and adjustment by the court.

When do I have to pay alimony?

Alimony, in some cases, is agreed to in a separation agreement. Some spouses prefer to admit fault and simply pay the other, as opposed to publicly "airing the dirty laundry." Another factor in providing for alimony in a separation agreement is attorney fees. If it appears clear that fault can be proven, and the spouse not at fault is dependent, an agreement can save attorney fees and costs of litigation.

A wife must show not only that she is dependent, but also that the husband is at fault to receive alimony.

There are defenses to fault. Fault on the part of both spouses is a defense, except in cases of adultery. Adultery on the part of the spouse seeking alimony is a defense to her claim.

Now that he has moved out, can I date?

If the wife is seeking alimony and she has sexual relations with another man prior to absolute divorce, that is adultery and if proven in court, will bar her claim to alimony. However, if the wife is not seeking alimony, her sexual relations are not related to her property claims. When the children are living in the home, and the sexual relations are occurring in the home, those acts may affect custody determinations.

In our example of John and Mary, John has, for a number of years, stayed out until one or two o'clock several nights a week, returning home with a strong odor of alcohol on his breath. Mary has begged him to change his behavior, but he refuses. Last month, John told Mary that he didn't love her anymore and moved out of the house. John is at fault in this situation. To receive alimony, Mary must show that she is economically dependent on John. Mary teaches school and makes substantially less than John. In addition, the lifestyle created during the marriage could not be maintained by Mary on her salary alone.

Nothing else appearing, Mary has a good potential claim for alimony.

However, after John left the home, Mary met Sam. Mary quickly became emotionally dependent on Sam who sympathized with her during this trying time. Sam asked Mary to go to Myrtle Beach with him for the weekend. Sam and Mary stayed in the same hotel room registered under Sam's name for two days.

Mary comes back to North Carolina and goes to see a lawyer. She admits to her lawyer that she has had a sexual relationship with Sam, and not only that she had sexual intercourse with Sam, but she has told her husband about the relationship in detail.

Mary's lawyer tells her that adultery is a bar to alimony. Mary blurts out that John has done it so often why can't she do the same thing. The answer is that John is not seeking support from Mary.

Will she get everything because I fooled around?

Adultery does not affect Mary's or John's claims for property distribution. You should always consult your lawyer to determine your potential liability but, unless there is a potential alimony claim, sexual relationships are not related to property claims.

Note that if custody is an issue, sexual relationships in the presence of the children is another matter.

What does fault mean?

Some of the grounds for permanent alimony are:

(1) Adultery.

(2) Commission of a criminal act.

(3) Spouse has engaged in an unnatural or abnormal sex act with a person of the same sex or different sex, or with a beast.

(4) Abandonment.

(5) Malicious turning out of the house.

(6) Cruel or barbarous treatment endangering the life of the spouse.

(7) Indignities.

(8) Spendthrift.

(9) Alcohol abuse.

(10) Failing to support with the necessities of life.

Ask your attorney if your case falls into one of these categories, but remember that your spouse must also be dependent to prevail against you in an alimony action.

In actions based on adultery the standard has become more difficult to prove. The spouse seeking temporary or permanent alimony must show both inclination and opportunity. The court has defined inclination as more than spending the night or staying until late in the same house or hotel with the alleged paramour. The standard requires other actions of the spouse and the paramour which show they had an inclination toward adultery, such as kissing in public or in front of third persons, or expressing more than a general affection for one another to a third person.

Suppose that John had not admitted his relationship with the alleged paramour, Susie, to his wife, Mary. Mary had become suspicious of John and hired a detective to find out if John was fooling around.

John and Mary had a long history of problems, including John's alcoholism. John had left the home and moved to a farm owned by his family in a rural county. After being hospitalized for alcoholism and psychiatric treatment, John returned to the home in an attempt to reconcile with Mary.

Prior to their separation, John had been chronically addicted to alcohol and more recently, had developed problems from the use of tranquilizers. John also verbally abused Mary, screaming at her that he did not love her and never had. He told her she was fat and old and he couldn't stand to touch her anymore, that he had always hated sex with her because she wasn't any good in bed. When John wasn't yelling at Mary, he refused to talk to her at all. He would go to a steak house and bring home one dinner, sit at the table and eat in front of her without offering her even a bite. Then he would get up, leave the house and stay gone for hours without ever telling her where he had been.

Occasionally, Mary would provoke John into acting in this manner. She would tell him that he was a failure and didn't want sex because he couldn't perform. That was true most of the time because of John's drug and alcohol abuse, but it was hurtful to John all the same.

John would get drunk, throw dishes and overturn furniture. Once he came into the kitchen and tried to pull off Mary's skirt. When she tried to get away, he socked her with his fist. Mary grabbed a pan from the stove and hit John on the head. John was almost knocked out, and Mary had to take him to the emergency room, where six stitches were required to close the gash in his forehead. Shortly thereafter, John moved to the farm.

Despite all the problems, Mary took him back after his treatment and agreed to try one more time. John did not resume his previous behavior, but Mary became suspicious and hired Joe Jolly, a private detective.

When John left on what was supposed to be an out-of-town business trip, Mary called the detective and told him which car he was driving. The detective suspected John might be found at his family's farm or at a condo his company owned in a nearby city.

The detective went to the farm in the early morning hours and saw John's car and another, later determined to be owned by Susie. The detective had driven past the farm house and parked in an orchard down the road. He walked back up the road and watched from behind a tree as John and Susie were leaving about 10:30 a.m. After watching for hours, he had seen no other persons enter or leave the house. Susie followed John out the driveway, each in their separate cars.

The detective followed them to a house in town, where they stayed until noon. Afterward, they left for a restaurant, where they remained for an hour.

Several days later, when John was again supposed to be out of town, the detective followed him to a motel, where John got a room. As the detective watched, the same woman who had been at the farmhouse arrived and went into John's room. John's and Susie's cars stayed at the motel throughout the night.

On a later occasion, the detective followed John to the company condo and watched again as Susie arrived to spend the night with him.

Using the evidence gathered by the detective, Mary sued for divorce and alimony based on his adultery. The jury returned a judgment in favor of Mary, but John appealed. The judgment was set aside by the Court of Appeals because while Mary had shown that John had an opportunity to commit adultery, she had not shown that he had an inclination to do so.

To some extent, this situation is based on a real case that came before the North Carolina Court of Appeals. The court stated that suspicion and conjecture were not enough to prove adultery. Being alone with a woman was not sufficient evidence, the court ruled. In modern society, said the jurists, adults follow widely diverse schedules of work and other activities throughout the day and night, and being alone together late at night is no more significant than being alone at any other time of the day.

Mary had shown only that John had the opportunity to engage in adultery. Her case might have been decided differently if she had shown that upon leaving the farm house, John had kissed Susie passionately and tweaked her bottom as she got into her car.

Mary might still win a claim for alimony , however, if she could show that John's actions were indignities against her. On the other hand, John might also claim that certain of Mary's actions were indignities to him. Indeed, actions of both might be labeled cruel and barbarous treatment. Indignities, cruel and barbarous treatment and alcohol abuse are all grounds for alimony.

Mary may have condoned some of John's behavior when she took him back, and as long as he doesn't resume that behavior, he could raise the defense that his former behavior was forgiven. But if John started drinking heavily again, or hit Mary, he could revive her claim.

CHAPTER 6
CHILD SUPPORT

How much child support am I entitled to receive? How much child support do I have to pay?

In July of 1990, new guidelines were set by North Carolina judges. Those guidelines were amended in July of 1991. North Carolina amends its guidelines each July. Updated guidelines are available at the Office of the Clerk of Court in each North Carolina county.

Prior to the new guidelines, child support was set on a percentage of the supporting spouse's income. For example, 25 percent for one child, 33 percent for two children, and so on. The percentages varied according to what the legislature decided was sufficient. These formulas based solely on the supporting spouse's income were determined by the legislature to be unfair and inequitable when the other spouse's income was not taken into account.

Next, I am going to give you an example of a particular fact situation and how child support can be determined in that situation.

Most of my clients have difficulty with following

the mathematics of the new method of computing child support. However, I wanted at least one example to help those who want to try to compute their own obligation.

If you are confused by the following example, that's because the new rules are confusing to the average person who is unfamiliar with them. Although the new rules allow for deviation, the following is a standard example representing no real person.

John and Mary have been married for sixteen years. John is now forty-one and Mary is thirty-eight. They have two children by this marriage. The eldest is a boy, John, Jr., age fifteen, and the youngest is a girl, Jane, age nine.

John has an income, before taxes and other deductions (gross income), of $38,000 per year. Mary has a gross income of $28,000 per year. The combined monthly gross income is as follows:

John's income per year	$38,000
Mary's income per year	$28,000
Combined annual income	$66,000
Combined income per month	$5,500
$66,000 ÷ 12 =	$5,500

To figure the percentage of income, divide the annual income of each parent by the combined annual income of $66,000, or $5,500 monthly.

$$\$38,000 \div 66,000 = .58$$

$$\$28,000 \div 66,000 = .42$$

John makes 58 percent of the total income and Mary makes 42 percent of the total income.

Upon separation, Mary wants physical custody of the children and will pay no daycare because both children are school age. According to the schedule, parents with two children should pay $1,135.00 combined for the two children's support. Mary should pay 42 percent and John should pay 58 percent of the $1,135.00. With no modifications, Mary will receive $638.30 per month for the two children, or $329.15 for each child.

$1,135.00	Scheduled support amount
x .42	Mary's percentage
$ 476.70	

$1,135.00	Scheduled support amount
x .58	John's percentage
$658.30	Amount John pays to Mary for support of the two minor children

If Jane, now nine, was age four and in daycare, an adjustment would be made for any daycare which was necessary for Mary to perform her job. If Jane's daycare expenses were $285.00 per month, 75 percent of that amount would be divided as an expense between Mary and John.

75 percent of $285.00 daycare equals $213.75.

Fifty-eight percent (58 percent) of the daycare would be paid by John using the percentage of income we already have established.

$213.75	
x .58	John's daycare obligation.

John's payment to Mary would then be increased by an additional percentage of the daycare:

$1,135.00	Scheduled amount
+ 213.75	Daycare
1,348.75	Total
x .58	John's percentage
$ 782.28	Total amount John pays Mary for support of two minor children, including daycare percentage

Other adjustments include health insurance premiums for the child or, in some cases, the parent's or child's unusual medical expenses and support payments for other children, to name a few.

Adjustments are also made in cases of multiple children living with separate spouses and children living in each separate household.

Instead of going into complicated mathematics, I want to answer your general questions. She and he are often interchangeable in these questions, depending on which parent is the primary care-giver.

I am often asked this question by men:

Why do I have to pay her when she doesn't spend it on the child?

The figures under the basic guideline include fixed expenses such as rent, utilities, even car payments.

What if she lives with her parents and has none of those expenses?

Although somebody has those expenses, this may be an adjustment factor. However, fictional rent can no longer be used as an expense. Fictional rent means rent that a parent lists as an expense that is in fact not paid, such as when a spouse paying child support lives with a parent who does not charge rent. The supporting spouse cannot claim as an expense what he or she would have paid if that spouse was paying rent. The situation is not the same when a spouse receiving support lives with a parent. The guideline support amount is determined on income of the parties. The expenses of the spouse receiving support are related to the support but the presumption is in favor of the guideline amount. In certain situations this presumption in favor of the guideline amount is helpful to a spouse receiving support who has been living on an income that was not enough to fully pay the expenses of that spouse and the child or children. It appears to be common for a separated or divorced spouse and the children to live with a parent. The grandparents then are paying a portion of the needs of the children in fixed expenses such as housing and other necessities. A requirement that the expenses of the custodial spouse, or the parent with the children, be actual expenses would trap that spouse in an economic situation that would be unresolvable.

Why can't he pay more if he lives with his parents and doesn't have any expenses?

I have never seen this increase a payment. However, a new case says he cannot use as an expense the amount he would pay in rent if he moved.

Can I get credit on court-ordered payments for amounts spent on clothing, food and other expenses for the child while the child is visiting with me?

In general, the answer is no, unless the custodial parent agrees. If the payment is made through the Clerk of Superior Court, the custodial parent will have to sign a receipt which is filed with the Clerk crediting payment in kind.

Do I have to pay child support while I have my child in the summer?

Yes. There is a provision in the new guidelines for reduction of the support. To receive an adjustment, a parent must physically have the child for one-third of the overnights in one full year. Summer visitation usually will not be sufficient.

How long will I have to pay child support?

Child support is payable until a child reaches the

age of 18, or until age 20 if that child still attends high school on a regular basis. In no event, except by agreement of the parties, shall child support continue after a child marries or dies. In some cases, a separation agreement can provide for child support that continues beyond age 18 or high school.

Will I have to pay for the college education of the child?

No, unless a separation agreement or other written agreement provides otherwise. An oral agreement is generally not sufficient to require one parent or the other to contribute to the college education of the children.

Can I put him in jail if he fails to pay?

Yes, eventually, if he fails to pay long enough. In order for a judge to put someone in jail, that person must be in contempt of court. Failure to pay under a court order is contempt if the person failing to pay has an ability to pay. Failure to pay under a separation agreement is not contempt if the court has not previously ordered the person to pay.

How can I make him pay?

By getting a court order. The order may be civil or criminal.

If Mary took out a warrant for John because he refused to pay support, she would be seeking a criminal order. In such an order, the district attorney's office would represent Mary as a prosecuting witness.

However, Mary cannot settle matters of custody, visitation or property rights by taking out a criminal warrant. If she hopes to receive more than minimal support, she probably should bring a civil action. The new guidelines and necessity for determining the income of both parents make calculating child support difficult at the criminal level. However, if a person looking for child support has no money for attorney fees, some expense can be saved by seeking an order in criminal court.

What if I think the child is not mine?

If a man thinks he is not the father of the child and the mother tries to seek support from him, he can ask for a blood test to determine paternity. These tests are extremely accurate. The father may ask for a blood test even if he is married to the mother. But, if the father is married to the mother, a presumption exists that the child is the child of the legal father. However, the court can find that he is not the father and does not have to pay support.

Can I make him pay through the court and have it deducted from his check?

Yes. It will take a court order, but a supporting spouse can be ordered to pay child support to the Clerk of Court and the court can order his employer to deduct the money from his or her wages and pay directly to the clerk's office. The clerk will then mail the money to the person receiving the support on behalf of the minor child. If he is supposed to be paying the money directly to the clerk and fails to pay, the clerk's office will bring him into court on charges of contempt. Both the person receiving support and the person paying support will then have to appear before a judge. The person paying support can tell the judge why he hasn't paid. If the judge finds that person able to pay, he can hold the person in contempt and possibly put him in jail.

• • • • •

Quick questions and answers covered under the new rules:

Are bonuses and commissions included in gross income for figuring child support? Yes.

Is the amount I pay to my pension plan included? Yes.

Are Social Security benefits included as income? Yes.

Is disability pay included as income? Yes.

Is self-employment income included? Yes, but it still appears to take some time and effort to determine exactly what amount is gross income when compared with expenses and tax deductions.

I am a housewife and my youngest child is three years old. Do I have to go to work to pay my share? No. (The same would be true for a male primary care-giver.)

My child is four years old. I still do not work. Will the court reduce my payment by the percentage of the amount I could have earned? Yes. If there is no employment history, the amount a person is capable of earning is the minimum hourly wage multiplied by a forty-hour week.

CHAPTER 7
CUSTODY AND VISITATION

North Carolina has two types of custody: legal and physical. Many men will tell me they want joint custody of their children. Women will say they want sole custody and to let him have visitation.

If he gets joint legal custody, will his child support be reduced?

In the earlier fact situation with John and Mary, John wants joint custody and Mary wants sole custody. John, Jr., is fifteen and Jane is nine. John says that the boy wants to live with his father instead of his mother.

In this situation, joint legal custody probably would not affect the matter of child support. Child support is controlled by the physical custody of the children, as opposed to the legal custody. Check with your tax preparer or read the IRS guidelines on who gets the deduction. In general, the parent with primary physical custody gets the deduction. Remember that the number of nights each parent has the child can be a factor in reducing child support. At this time, a parent must have the child at least one-third of the overnights in a year to reduce or eliminate the support.

When do I need sole legal custody?

If one parent has a fear that the other parent will remove the child from the state in a joint legal custody agreement, that fear should be addressed in either sole custody in one parent or an order requiring the parent to limit out-of-state transportation of the child. If there is no agreement or order as to custody, both parents have equal rights to the control of the child, including taking the child out of state.

A presumption exists in the North Carolina statutes in favor of joint legal custody. Many fathers now seek that designation. I believe that many men mistakenly believe that the designation will reduce child support. It will not.

What is the difference between joint legal custody and joint physical custody?

As described in the chapter on custody, joint physical custody requires an adjustment in child support only if the shared arrangement amounts to one-third of the overnights in a year and is something more than simply extended visitation. The day-night mathematical designation is not enough by itself. The days in the full year must also be counted and not shorter periods such as a month or a summer.

When can I stop paying support I don't believe I owe?

Be aware that once an order or agreement has been entered, a change in that order or agreement is necessary. Do not stop paying because you just think you do not owe the money.

A parent paying child support can be held in contempt of court and jailed if that parent fails to pay support.

Examples of situations in which the parent has an inability to pay are medical disability or loss of employment, both of which may be a defense to contempt of court based on an inability to pay. The best practice is for a parent who is making child support payments to move the court to reduce the payment should a change of circumstances occur.

Past-due payments will continue to accumulate if no order is entered.

Will my children have to testify?

In my example of John, Mary, John, Jr., and Jane, Mary would not agree to give John joint legal custody or physical custody of John, Jr. John, Jr. was called to testify at the hearing. The judge decided that John, Jr., was old enough to express his desires. In this case, John, Jr., testified in open court as any other witness. In many cases, children will be allowed to testify or state their feelings in the judge's office or "chambers". In some cases, the lawyers or parents will be allowed to listen in, and in others, they will not be allowed to listen. The preference of the judge, and sensitivity and age of the children are usually controlling factors.

In our case, Jane was not interviewed by the judge. Neither parent indicated that she had expressed a strong preference and both the judge and lawyers felt she was a little too young to be asked to choose between her parents in this manner. I use the expression "choose between the parents" specifically because many children feel that they are being asked to make a choice between their parents and do not want to "hurt the feelings" of either parent. I prefer that this be avoided. In some cases, this situation cannot be avoided. I suggest counselling of the child, both before and after court. The child must understand that both parents want the best for the child and that the parent who does not retain physical control will not reject the child.

A word of warning here. Parents do sometimes reject their children in these situations, and children do reject parents. Parents, be careful of your motives – you may get more than you ask.

Older children are, of course, more likely to be placed according to their wishes. John and Mary got joint legal custody of both children. The judge said it appeared to him that both John and Mary were fit and proper parents. John received physical custody of John, Jr., and Mary received physical custody of Jane.

In this case, an adjustment would be made under the guidelines for the support of the children. If you are adventurous, you might want to compute the figures using the incomes in the earlier example.

What if I want him to have standard visitation?

Both parents in John's and Mary's case received a standard visitation, with emphasis on the children being in the same home on holidays and as often as possible. Visitation schedules seem to vary between court districts. Most involve an every-other weekend situation from Friday after work until Sunday evening. The party seeking visitation is usually responsible for the transportation of the child, although this often varies in different circumstances. Having the children on alternate holidays is also fairly standard. For instance, one parent may have Easter one year. The other parent will receive it the next year. Birthdays are alternated in the same manner. The mother usually has the children for Mother's Day, and the father usually has them for Father's Day. Christmas is a longer holiday and divided in the same manner. One year, one parent will have the children from the time school is out for the holiday until, for instance, 2:00 p.m. on Christmas Day. The next year, the other parent will have that time period. The second parent would then have the child or children until the end of school break.

This schedule is, of course, open to amendments if the parents can agree peacefully. It sometimes becomes difficult for children to be with their grandparents, cousins, aunts, uncles, etc., if there is no flexibility between the parents. A parent who refuses to abide by a court-ordered schedule, despite the wishes of the other parent, can be held in contempt of court and possibly sanctioned by the court.

Does joint custody mean the children are to be with me as much as they are with their mother?

A case of true joint physical custody of the children is not common. However, joint physical custody is more common than in the past. Some parents agree to share physical custody on a week-by-week basis. School and transportation problems can obviously arise. Courts can order this alternative if it appears to be in the best interest of the children. Some parents work well with this type of arrangement. Some parents cannot deal with shared physical custody and the logistical problems thereby created. Parents who contemplate this type arrangement should be aware of the demands for communication and flexibility.

If I let him see the children, can I make him bring them back?

It depends on whether a custody order has been entered or the spouses have agreed on custody in a separation agreement or other written agreement. Neither spouse has any greater right to the physical custody of the children until a custody determination is made between the spouses in writing or by order of the court.

For example, John and Mary separated and Mary took out a warrant for John because he refused to pay child support. John had refused to pay because Mary would not let him visit with the children. Mary and John went to court and John was ordered to pay child support. The next day, John went to the children's school and picked them up. Mary called the police and demanded that they get the children from John. The police told Mary that they could not do that because John had as much right to custody as she, unless she had a written agreement or court order that said otherwise.

If he takes the children can I get them back?

A court can grant an emergency order on custody. Say that Mary went to an lawyer and filed an action for custody. A hearing was held two weeks later and a temporary custody determination was made until a final agreement could be made. If John had threatened to remove the children from the state or Mary had reason to believe that John would physically harm the children, Mary might have been entitled to an emergency order returning the children, at least on a temporary basis, to her physical custody.

What if he does take the children out of the state?

If one spouse removes the child from the state and no custody determination has been made, the other spouse can go get the children, if he or she can do so peacefully. Before attempting to retrieve children in this manner, it is best to consult a lawyer.

CHAPTER 8
STEPPARENTS

An entire book could be written concerning the psychology of dealing as a stepparent. I am not a psychologist but I can answer some of your legal questions.

As a stepparent, do I have any legal responsibility to my stepchildren?

Stepparents have little legal control of their stepchildren and a great deal of legal responsibility. In the criminal law, a person in loco parentis may be held to the same punishment for committing a crime against the child as would the natural parent. A person living in the home for an extended period without marriage may be held to this same standard.

Do I have to support his children?

A stepparent is not responsible for payment of child support. However, the income of that spouse may be used to determine the ability of the parent to pay support. A natural parent's first obligation is, of course, to the child or children. The obligation to support a spouse comes second.

In reality, many stepparents contribute financial support to the children of their spouses. The children may live in the household, or the stepparent may actually provide money to make support payments for children residing with their spouse's former spouse.

What can we do about his ex-wife harassing us?

Situations arise where a divorced spouse becomes jealous of the stepparent or sees that person's role as an infringement on parenting rights. Courts generally do not approve of a parent teaching a child that the stepparent is its father or mother in lieu of his or her natural parent. The problem may arise as to what a child calls a stepparent.

To avoid conflict, a distinction should be made between the term the child uses for a natural parent. I think this varies with the age and situation. Preference should be given to the choice the natural parent wishes to be called by the child. This problem appears to arise more with fathers.

Mothers and stepmothers seem to come in conflict in matters of discipline. There are no "rules" to resolve these problems. In fact, some cannot be resolved because the underlying emotion of the parent, stepparent or the children, is the true problem and not the behavior of the parent or stepparent. I have seen families establish behaviors or disciplines or rules for each household that the children abide by when they are in that household.

Problems can arise here also if the parents communicate solely through the children and receive a view the child wants to portray. Children are capable of manipulation and often succeed. If you have expressed a dislike for a stepparent, the child may see an easy villain to be used to get the child's way. The child may even sense this feeling on your part if you have been one of those unusual parents who does not criticize your ex-spouse or his or her new family. A stepparent may have to endure being portrayed as the villain to keep the new family from falling apart under these pressures. Another common problem arises when a parent requests or subpoenas the stepparent's income for purposes of determining child support. I have already indicated that a stepparent is not required to contribute to the support of a stepchild. However, the stepparent's income is necessary to determine the expenses of the household and the parent's ability to provide for his own support. Cooperation in furnishing this information can only help the situation. Cooperation can also reduce attorney fees. If a stepparent or parent fails to voluntarily furnish this information the court will order the parent or employer of the parent to produce that information.

CHAPTER 9
ATTORNEY FEES

If your attorney does not bring up the subject of cost, ask about it. Most child support, custody, and alimony litigation is done on an hourly basis. Generally, a non-refundable retainer is charged by the attorney. Although the attorney may, in some cases, credit the hourly rate toward the initial retainer, if you reconcile with your spouse, or decide you want another attorney, or for any other reason you do not go forward with the action, you generally will not get the retainer refunded.

How much am I going to have to pay in attorney fees?

Hourly rates for lawyers usually also include minimum charges for phone calls and correspondence. If you call the attorney at home, you will usually find a double charge, if not more than double. Unless a true emergency arises, you will receive better service if you contact your lawyer during office hours. The lawyer does not take your file home. The file is at the office.

Can I collect attorney fees from my spouse?

In cases of child support, custody, or contempt, one spouse may be required to contribute to the attorney fees of the other spouse. Unfortunately, judges in North Carolina generally fail to award a fee substantial enough to cover the entire fee. Your attorney may explain this to you and request that you pay the entire fee and wait for reimbursement under the judge's order. Some attorneys will allow a spouse to pay a partial fee and agree to let the attorney keep the court-ordered fee in addition to the retainer.

Whatever your fee arrangement is with your attorney, make sure you understand that agreement. You should feel comfortable enough to ask about the cost and also to request that agreement in writing. Most attorneys are pleased to have a written agreement concerning the fee.

Will my legal insurance cover this attorney fee?

Some companies in North Carolina are now offering legal insurance as a benefit. Legal insurance is generally low in cost and good to have if you need it. Legal expenses are seldom planned for and are not a budgeted item. Insurance, or a payment plan with the attorney, can help this problem. However, most attorneys require the payment in advance of the services. In longer cases, monthly or bi-monthly billing may be used. In this situation, no further work is done by the attorney if the bill is unpaid. If you are on a billing method, request regular billing so you do not get into a cost that is more than you anticipated or more than you can pay.

I strongly encourage clients to obtain legal insurance if it is available to them. Legal expenses, like medical expenses, are generally large expenses which can exhaust your savings or break your budget. Legal services also often are not available if you cannot pay for them.

DEFINITIONS

A. Income

For the purpose of these Guidelines, "income" is defined as actual gross income of the parent, if employed to full capacity, or potential income if unemployed or underemployed. Gross income of each parent should be determined as specified below.

(1) Gross income. Gross income includes income from any source, except as excluded below, and includes but is not limited to income from salaries, wages, commissions, bonuses, dividends, severance pay, pensions, interest, trust income, annuities, capital gains, social security benefits, workers compensation benefits, unemployment insurance benefits, disability pay and insurance benefits, gifts, prizes and alimony or maintenance received from persons other than the parties to the instant action. While includable as income, non-recurring, one-time payments should be distinguished from ongoing income.

Specifically excluded are benefits received from means-tested public assistance programs, including but not limited to Aid to Families with Dependent Children (AFDC), Supplemental Security Income

(SSI), Food Stamps and General Assistance.

(2) Income from self-employment or operation of a business. For income from self-employment, rent, royalties, proprietorship of a business, or joint ownership of a partnership or closely held corporation, gross income is defined as gross receipts minus ordinary and necessary expenses required for self-employment or business operation. Specifically excluded from ordinary and necessary expenses for purposes of these Guidelines are amounts allowable by the Internal Revenue Service for the accelerated component of depreciation expenses, investment tax credits, or any other business expenses determined by the Court to be inappropriate for determining gross income for purposes of calculating child support. In general, income and expenses from self-employment or operation of a business should be reviewed to determine an appropriate level of gross income available to the parent to satisfy a child support obligation. In most cases, this amount will differ from a determination of business income for tax purposes.

Expense reimbursements or in-kind payments received by a parent in the course of employment, self-employment, or operation of a business should be counted as income if they are significant and reduce personal living expenses. Such payments might include a company car, free housing, or reimbursement meals.

(3) Potential income. If a parent is voluntarily

unemployed or underemployed, child support shall be calculated based on determination of potential income, except that a determination of potential income should not be made for a parent who is physically or mentally incapacitated or is caring for a very young child (one who has not yet reached its third birthday) for whom the parents owe a joint legal responsibility.

Determination of potential income shall be made by determining employment potential and probable earnings level based on the obligator's recent work history, occupational qualifications and prevailing job opportunities and earning levels in the community. If there is no recent work history and no higher education or vocational training, it is suggested that income be imputed at least at the minimum hourly wage for a 40-hour work week.

(4) Income verification. Income statements of the parents should be verified with documentation of both the current and past income. Suitable documentation of current earnings (at least one full month) includes pay stubs, employer statements, or receipts and expenses if self-employed. Documentation of current income must be supplemented with copies of the most recent tax return to provide verification of earnings over a longer period. Sanctions may be imposed for failure to comply with this provision on the motion of either party or by the Court on its own motion.

B. Pre-existing Child Support Obligations and Responsibility for Other Children.

The amount(s) of any pre-existing court order(s) for child support or amount paid per separation agreement(s) should be deducted from gross income to the extent payment is actually made under such order(s) or agreement(s).

The amount of financial responsibility a parent has for his or her children currently residing in the household who are not involved in this action should be deducted from gross income. Use of the adjustment is appropriate at the time of the establishment of a child support order in a proceeding to modify an existing order. However, in a proceeding to modify, it may not be the sole basis for a reduction. The adjustment applies only to a party's natural or adopted children.

The amount to be subtracted from monthly gross income for the responsibility of other children is the amount listed in the Schedule of Basic Child Support Obligations which would represent support obligation based only on the responsible parent's gross income, without any other adjustments, for the number of children for whom the parent is also responsible.

Actual payments of alimony should not be considered as a deduction from gross income but may be considered as a factor to vary from the final presumptive child support obligation.

C. Health Insurance

For each child support order, consideration should be given to provision of adequate health insurance coverage for the child. Such health insurance should normally be provided by the parent that can obtain the most comprehensive coverage through an employer at least cost.

If either parent does carry health insurance for the child(ren) due support, the cost of that coverage for that parent and children only should be deducted from that parent's gross income. If coverage is provided through an employer, only the employee's portion of cost should be deducted. In no event shall costs incurred for insuring a subsequent spouse of either party be deducted from that party's income.

D. Basic Child Support Obligation

The basic child support obligation is determined using the Schedule of Basic Child Support Obligations available from the Clerk of Court. For combined monthly adjusted gross income amounts falling between amounts shown in the schedule, basic child support amounts should be extrapolated.

The number of children refers to children for whom the parents share joint legal responsibility and for whom support is being sought.

E. Child Care Costs

Considering federal child care tax credits, 75% of child care cost incurred due to employment or job search for such is added to the basic obligation. Such child care costs must be reasonable.

F. Extraordinary Expenses

The Court may make adjustments for extraordinary expenses and order payments for such term and in such manner as the Court deems necessary. Extraordinary medical expenses include, but are not limited to, such costs as are reasonably necessary for orthodonture, dental treatment, asthma treatments, physical therapy and any uninsured chronic health problem. At the discretion of the Court, professional counseling or psychiatric therapy for diagnosed mental disorders may also be considered as an extraordinary medical expense. Payments for such expenses shall be apportioned in the same manner as the basic child support obligation and ordered paid as the Court deems equitable.

Other extraordinary expenses are added to the basic child support obligation. Other extraordinary expenses include:

(1) Any expenses for attending any special or private elementary or secondary schools to meet the particular educational needs of the child.

(2) Any expenses for transportation of the child between the homes of the parents.

APPENDIX A

The North Carolina Child Support Guidelines, promulgated by the conference of Chief District Court Judges, are published jointly by the North Carolina Administrative Office of the Courts and the Department of Human Resources in accordance with G.S. 50-13.4 (c). Copies of these Guidelines are available from the offices of the Clerk of Superior Court. For information regarding the use of the Child Support Guidelines, please refer to G.S. 50-13.4 (c).

APPENDIX B

The forms listed below are available from the office of the Clerk of Superior Court to aid in the computation of the child support obligation:

AOC-CV-627 – Worksheet A, Child Support Obligation, Sole Custody

AOC-CV-628 – Worksheet B, Child Support Obligation, Joint or Shared Physical Custody

AOC-CV-629 – Worksheet C, Child Support Obligation, Split Custody.